W9-BIJ-288

Dinosaurs

School Specialty Publishing

This edition published by School Specialty Publishing,
a member of the School Specialty Family.

© 2007 Twin Sisters IP, LLC. All Rights Reserved.

Send inquiries to:
School Specialty Publishing
8720 Orion Place
Columbus, Ohio 43240-2111

3 4 5 6 7 8 9 10 WAF 10 09 08 07

Credits:
Publisher: Twin Sisters Productions, LLC
Executive Producers: Kim Mitzo Thompson, Karen Mitzo Hilderbrand
Music Arranged by: Hal Wright
Workbook Author: Ken Carder
Illustrations: Lon Eric Craven
Workbook Design: Steven Dewitt

ISBN: 0-7696-4578-X

What Is a Dinosaur?

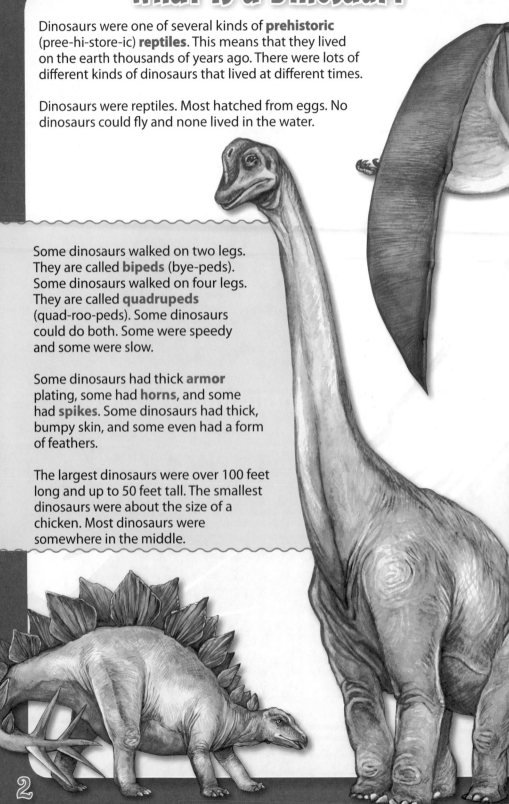

Dinosaurs were one of several kinds of **prehistoric** (pree-hi-store-ic) **reptiles**. This means that they lived on the earth thousands of years ago. There were lots of different kinds of dinosaurs that lived at different times.

Dinosaurs were reptiles. Most hatched from eggs. No dinosaurs could fly and none lived in the water.

Some dinosaurs walked on two legs. They are called **bipeds** (bye-peds). Some dinosaurs walked on four legs. They are called **quadrupeds** (quad-roo-peds). Some dinosaurs could do both. Some were speedy and some were slow.

Some dinosaurs had thick **armor** plating, some had **horns**, and some had **spikes**. Some dinosaurs had thick, bumpy skin, and some even had a form of feathers.

The largest dinosaurs were over 100 feet long and up to 50 feet tall. The smallest dinosaurs were about the size of a chicken. Most dinosaurs were somewhere in the middle.

Most dinosaurs were **herbivores** (her-bih-vores). This means they ate plants. The three-horned dinosaur Triceratops was a plant-eating dinosaur.

Some dinosaurs were **carnivores** (car-nih-vores). This means they ate meat. The huge dinosaur Tyrannosaurus rex was a meat-eating dinosaur.

Dinosaurs mysteriously went **extinct** (ex-stink-t). This means that they have all died and are gone forever. Scientists have many **theories**, or ideas, about what happened to the dinosaurs. No one knows for sure what caused the dinosaurs to die out.

It is very difficult to figure out what noises the dinosaurs made, how they behaved, how they mated, or what colors they were. Scientists called **paleontologists** (pay-lee-on-tall-oh-gists) study **fossils** (fahs-sils). Fossils are what remain today of things that lived many, many years ago. These remains have become part of the rocks buried in the earth. Fossils include tracks or footprints, bones, skin, and even eggs.

Who Named the Dinosaurs?

The word dinosaur means *fearfully great lizard*. A scientist named Sir Richard Owen from Great Britain first used the word *dinosaur* in 1842. In Greek, *deinos* means *fearfully great* and *sauros* means *lizard*.

Dinosaurs are named by the people who discover the fossils or by the paleontologist who determines that the fossils represent a new kind of dinosaur. Sometimes, the dinosaur's name describes something unusual about its body, head, or feet. Some are named for the location where they are found. And some dinosaurs are named for the way scientists think the dinosaurs behaved. The names have to be approved by the **International Commission on Zoological Nomenclature**.

©2007 Twin Sisters IP, LLC. All Rights Reserved.

Dinosaur Scramble

The clues will help you unscramble the following words.

SPTREILE Dinosaurs belonged to this group of animals.

Reptiles

ISONALEOTTPLOG This scientist studies dinosaurs and other fossils.

LIFOSSS All that remain of the dinosaurs bodies today are these hard, rock-like objects.

VOBRHERIE Most dinosaurs ate plants.

NIVOCARRE Some dinosaurs were meat-eaters.

TXNICTE All the dinosaurs have died and are gone forever.

PEDBI Some dinosaurs walked on two legs.

DPEDRUQUA Some dinosaurs walked on four legs.

ULFRFEALY REGAT ZLIRDA The meaning of the word *dinosaur*.

©2007 Twin Sisters IP, LLC. All Rights Reserved

4

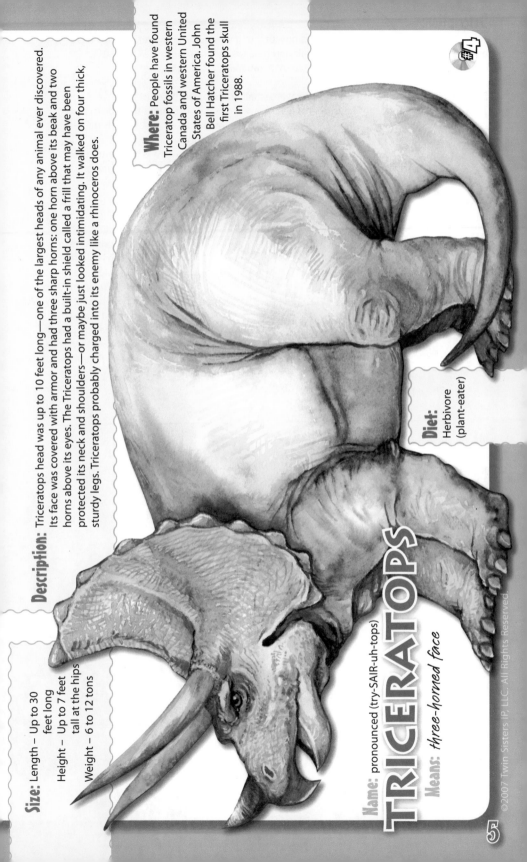

Where: People have found Triceratop fossils in western Canada and western United States of America. John Bell Hatcher found the first Triceratops skull in 1988.

Description: Triceratops head was up to 10 feet long—one of the largest heads of any animal ever discovered. Its face was covered with armor and had three sharp horns: one horn above its beak and two horns above its eyes. The Triceratops had a built-in shield called a frill that may have been protected its neck and shoulders—or maybe just looked intimidating. It walked on four thick, sturdy legs. Triceratops probably charged into its enemy like a rhinoceros does.

Diet: Herbivore (plant-eater)

Size: Length – Up to 30 feet long

Height – Up to 7 feet tall at the hips

Weight – 6 to 12 tons

Name: pronounced (try-SAIR-uh-tops)

TRICERATOPS

Means: three-horned face

©2007 Twin Sisters IP, LLC. All Rights Reserved.

Description:

Tyrannosaurus rex wasn't the biggest dinosaur, but it was huge. However, its arms were only about 3 feet long, and it had two-fingered hands. Tyrannosaurus rex had 50 cone-shaped, sharp teeth—some the size of a banana.

Because its arms were short and its eyes were small, some paleontologists believe Tyrannosaurus rex may not have been a fierce, savage predator. It might have been a **scavenger**. This means that it ate animals that were already dead. Tyrannosaurus rex may have bullied or scared away carnivorous dinosaurs after they had killed their prey. Then, it would have stolen their food.

Where:

Someone found the first Tyrannosaurus rex in Hell Creek, Montana. People have found a total of 30 incomplete fossils of Tyrannosaurus rex in the United States of America, Canada, and Mongolia. People have even found Tyrannosaurus rex dung!

Diet:

Carnivore
(meat-eater)

Size:

Length – 40 feet long
Height – 15 to 20 feet tall
Weight – 5 to 7 tons

Name: pronounced
(tye-RAN-uh-SAWR-us)

TYRANNOSAURUS REX

Means: *tyrant lizard king*

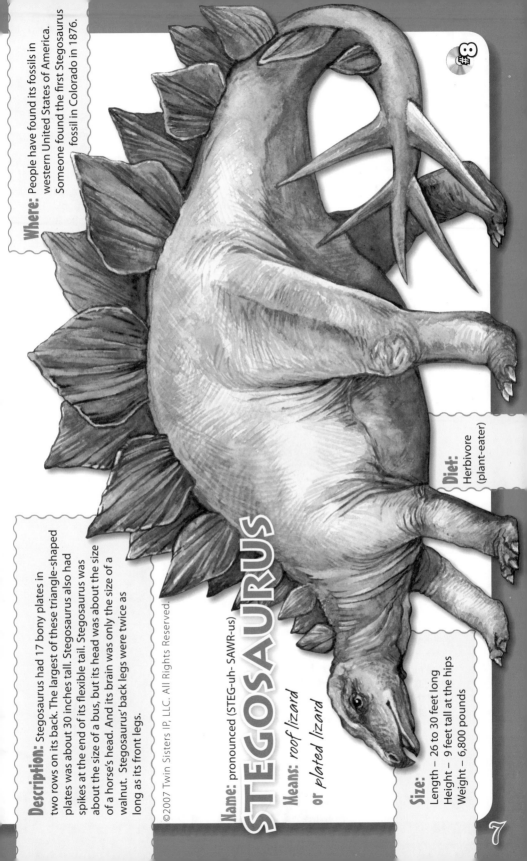

Where: People have found its fossils in western United States of America. Someone found the first Stegosaurus fossil in Colorado in 1876.

Diet: Herbivore (plant-eater)

Description: Stegosaurus had 17 bony plates in two rows on its back. The largest of these triangle-shaped plates was about 30 inches tall. Stegosaurus also had spikes at the end of its flexible tail. Stegosaurus was about the size of a bus, but its head was about the size of a horse's head. And its brain was only the size of a walnut. Stegosaurus' back legs were twice as long as its front legs.

©2007 Twin Sisters IP, LLC. All Rights Reserved.

Name: pronounced (STEG-uh- SAWR-us)

STEGOSAURUS

Means: *roof lizard*
or *plated lizard*

Size:
Length – 26 to 30 feet long
Height – 9 feet tall at the hips
Weight – 6,800 pounds

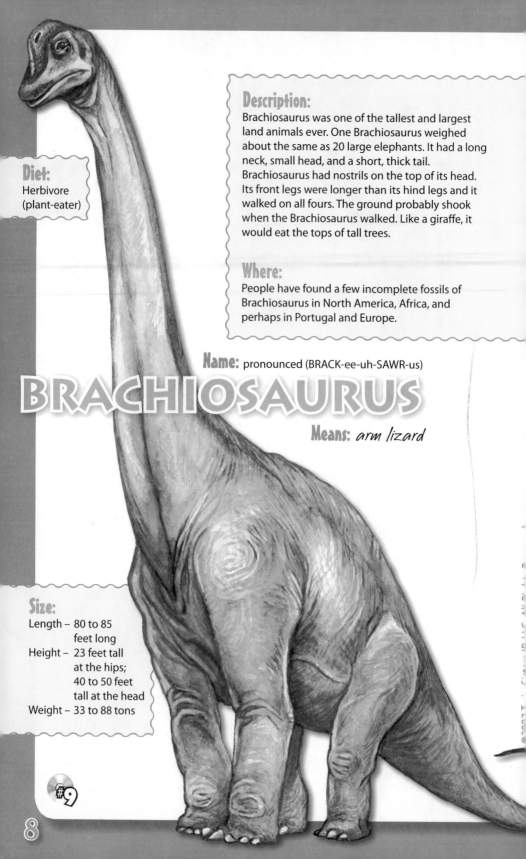

Diet:
Herbivore
(plant-eater)

Description:
Brachiosaurus was one of the tallest and largest
land animals ever. One Brachiosaurus weighed
about the same as 20 large elephants. It had a long
neck, small head, and a short, thick tail.
Brachiosaurus had nostrils on the top of its head.
Its front legs were longer than its hind legs and it
walked on all fours. The ground probably shook
when the Brachiosaurus walked. Like a giraffe, it
would eat the tops of tall trees.

Where:
People have found a few incomplete fossils of
Brachiosaurus in North America, Africa, and
perhaps in Portugal and Europe.

Name: pronounced (BRACK-ee-uh-SAWR-us)

BRACHIOSAURUS

Means: *arm lizard*

Size:
Length – 80 to 85
          feet long
Height – 23 feet tall
          at the hips;
          40 to 50 feet
          tall at the head
Weight – 33 to 88 tons

#9

8

Name: pronounced (plee-zee-oh-SAWR-us)

PLESIOSAURUS

Means: *near lizard*

Diet:
Carnivore – fish, octopus, and other swimming animals

Where:
North America, Europe, and Australia

Description: Plesiosaurus was not a dinosaur. It was a marine reptile.

Plesiosaurus had a small, short head, a long, snake-like neck, a broad, solid body, and a short tail. Its sharp interlocking teeth were well equipped for catching fish. Its four paddle-like legs were similar to the legs of a marine turtle.

Size:
Length – 10 to 60 feet
Weight – about 200 pounds

©2007 Twin Sisters IP, LLC. All Rights Reserved.

Name: pronounced (komp-sog-NAY-thus)

COMPSOGNATHUS

Means: *pretty jaw*

Description: Compsognathus is one of the smallest-known dinosaurs. It was about the size of a chicken. Compsognathus walked on two long, thin legs. It had three-toed feet, a small, pointed head, small, sharp teeth, hollow bones, and a long, flexible neck. Compsognathus had short arms with two clawed fingers on each hand. Its long tail helped it to stay balanced as it moved.

Where: People have found its fossils in Germany and France.

Size:
Length – 2–5 feet long
Height – 10 inches tall at the hips
Weight – 6 ½ pounds

Diet:
Carnivore
(meat-eater)

©2007 Twin Sisters IP, LLC. All Rights Reserved.

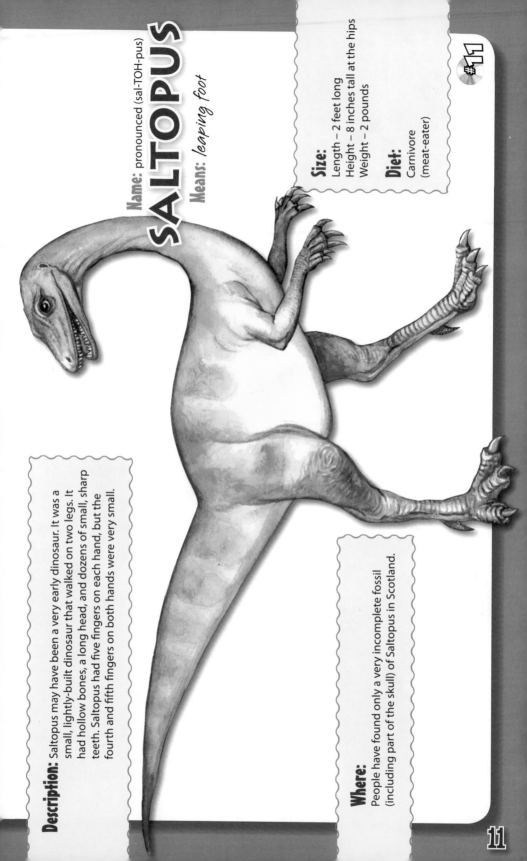

Name: pronounced (sal-TOH-pus)

SALTOPUS

Means: *leaping foot*

Size:
Length – 2 feet long
Height – 8 inches tall at the hips
Weight – 2 pounds

Diet:
Carnivore
(meat-eater)

Description: Saltopus may have been a very early dinosaur. It was a small, lightly-built dinosaur that walked on two legs. It had hollow bones, a long head, and dozens of small, sharp teeth. Saltopus had five fingers on each hand, but the fourth and fifth fingers on both hands were very small.

Where: People have found only a very incomplete fossil (including part of the skull) of Saltopus in Scotland.

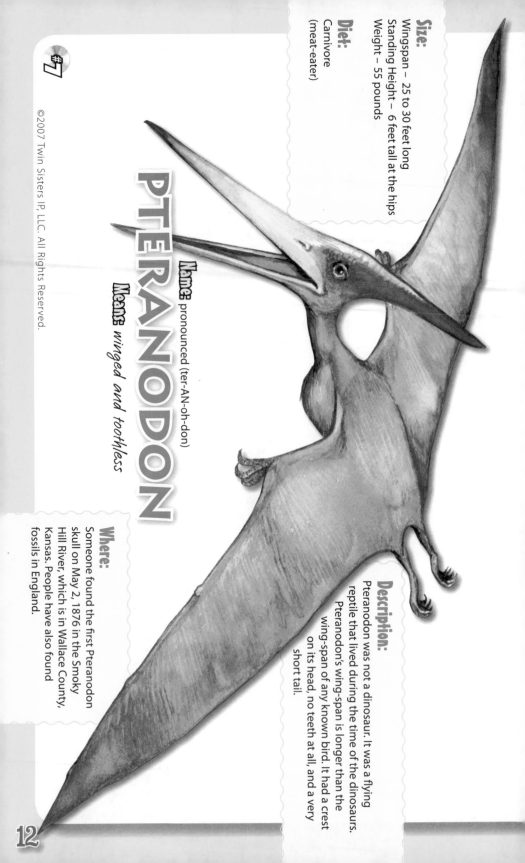

Size:
Wingspan – 25 to 30 feet long
Standing Height – 6 feet tall at the hips
Weight – 55 pounds

Diet:
Carnivore
(meat-eater)

#7

©2007 Twin Sisters IP, LLC. All Rights Reserved.

Name: pronounced (ter-AN-oh-don)

PTERANODON

Means *winged and toothless*

Where:
Someone found the first Pteranodon skull on May 2, 1876 in the Smoky Hill River, which is in Wallace County, Kansas. People have also found fossils in England.

Description:
Pteranodon was not a dinosaur. It was a flying reptile that lived during the time of the dinosaurs. Pteranodon's wing-span is longer than the wing-span of any known bird. It had a crest on its head, no teeth at all, and a very short tail.

12

Description:

Giganotosaurus was longer than Tyrannosaurus rex! It walked on two legs and it had a 6-foot-long skull, a brain the size of a banana, and enormous jaws with 8-inch-long teeth.

Where:

Someone first found Giganotosaurus in 1994 in southern Argentina, South America.

©2007 Twin Sisters IP, LLC. All Rights Reserved.

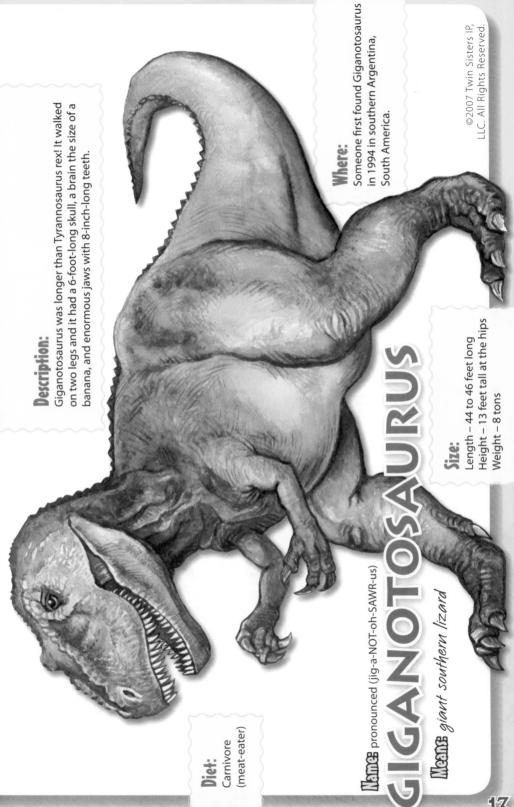

GIGANOTOSAURUS

Name: pronounced (jig-a-NOT-oh-SAWR-us)

Means: *giant southern lizard*

Size:
Length – 44 to 46 feet long
Height – 13 feet tall at the hips
Weight – 8 tons

Diet:
Carnivore
(meat-eater)

Description:

Ichthyosaurus was not a dinosaur. It was a marine reptile.

Ichthyosaurus had sharp teeth, long jaws, and big eyes. It had four crescent-shaped fins, a dorsal fin, and a fish-like tail. Ichthyosaurus breathed air with lungs through nostrils which were close to the eyes near the top of the snout. It had to come to the surface of the water to breathe air.

Ichthyosaurus gave birth to live young. People have found the fossil of Ichthyosaurus with babies in its abdomen.

Size:

Length – 7 to 30 feet long

Weight – about 200 pounds

Diet:

Carnivore – fish, octopus, and other swimming animals

ICHTHYOSAURUS

Name: pronounced (ICk-thee-oh-SAWR-us)

Means: *fish lizard*

Where:

People have found Ichthyosaurus fossils in North and South America and in Europe.

©2007 Twin Sisters IP, LLC. All Rights Reserved.

#11

Name: **ALLOSAURUS**

pronounced (AL-uh-SAWR-us)

Means: *different lizard*

Diet:
Carnivore (meat-eater)

Size:
Length - about 40 feet long
Height - 10 feet tall at the hips
Weight - up to 4 ½ tons

Description:
Allosaurus was a predator with a huge head, an S-shaped neck, short arms, three-fingered hands, and sharp claws that were up to 6 inches long. It had two short horns as well as bony knobs and ridges above its eyes and on the top of its head. It had large, powerful jaws with long, sharp teeth that were 2 to 4 inches long. Allosaurus got its name from its unusual backbone. The bones in its back were lighter than the bones of other dinosaurs.

Where:
People have found over 60 Allosaurus fossils in places such as western United States of America, Portugal, Europe, Africa, and Australia. Someone discovered the first almost complete Allosaurus skeleton in Colorado in 1883.

©2007 Twin Sisters IP, LLC. All Rights Reserved.

Name: pronounced (KWET-zal-koh-AT-lus)

QUETZALCOATLUS

named after the Aztec feathered god Quetzalcoat

Description:
Quetzalcoatlus was a flying reptile. It was the largest flying animal ever found. It had hollow bones and a small body. Its legs and neck were very long. Quetzalcoatlus had a large brain and big eyes. Its body may have been covered with fur or fuzz. A leather-like membrane covered Quetzalcoatlus' wings, which were nearly 9 inches thick at the elbow.

Size:
Wingspan – Nearly 36 feet long!
Neck – 10 feet long
Legs – 7 feet long
Weight – Up to 300 pounds

Diet:
Carnivore – skimmed the water to find prey

©2007 Twin Sisters IP, LLC. All Rights Reserved.

Design Your Own Dinosaur!

Start with the doodle below and create a dinosaur!
Add a head and legs! Will your dinosaur have a long
or short tail? Spikes or horns? Scales or feathers?

©2007 Twin Sisters IP, LLC. All Rights Reserved.

Prehistoric Dig!

Find each of the dinosaurs and prehistoric reptiles that
are listed below. Search horizontally, vertically, or diagonally.

Stegosaurus   Plesiosaurus   Triceratops
Giganotosaurus   Pteranodon   Allosaurus
Saltopus   Brachiosaurus   Compsognathus
Tyrannosaurus rex   Ichthyosaurus   Quetzalcoatlus

```
O E S I O O H A L L O S A U N A D I O N
U O O P L E S I O S A U R U S E S A P L
A L T B E C O M P S O G N A T H U S T I
X U T Y R A N N O S A U R U S R E X E A
B P G U R S G O A S S S O T N N S U R R
R I T I I A I I S L S L R A U T S R A U
A C A S G R N I G G L U R A O U T S N U
C H T U A A N T A A O S U L S E A O U
H T S Z Q U N G O S N O S T E G L T C
I H T A H S O O O S I O A A N A O T R T
O Y R U L L N I T H A O T U U I S O A U
S O I S N T S C C O C U R O T R A G T U
A S C S O E O A H L S U R P S U U C R R
U A E R L H R P A A A A M U P A R S N A
R U R P S B N Z U S G E U O S U U O D O
U I A Q H U T U O S D U G R P A S R S R
S A T U B E U G P T E R A N O D O N U L
S O O O U P E T R I C E R A T B R C M S
A S P Q I T I C H T H Y O S A U R U S B
U O S A S U R O O U N U U T O S R R H U
```

Solution - pg. 26

©2007 Twin Sisters IP, LLC. All Rights Reserved.

18

Coffee Ground Fossils

#2

Make your own prehistoric fossils overnight!

What you will need:

- 1 cup of used coffee grounds
- 1/2 cup of cold coffee
- 1 cup of flour
- 1/2 cup of salt
- Waxed paper
- Mixing bowl

- Small objects to make impressions in the dough
- Empty can or a butter knife
- Toothpicks (optional)
- String to hang your fossil (optional)

Mix together the coffee grounds, cold coffee, flour, and salt. Knead the dough and then flatten it out onto the waxed paper. Cut out circles of the dough with a can. Or, use the dull knife to cut pieces large enough to fit your "fossil" objects. Press your objects firmly into the dough. When you take the object out, you will have your fossil impression. If you want to hang the fossil, poke a hole through the circle near the edge. Poke the string through the hole and tie together the ends. Let the fossil dry overnight and then hang it for everybody to see.

Possible Fossil Objects

- **Small plastic dinosaurs**
- **Dog biscuits**
- **Leftover chicken bones**
- **Shells from peanuts or walnuts**
- **Coins**

©2007 Twin Sisters IP, LLC. All Rights Reserved.

Homemade Dinosaur Bones

Make your own dinosaur bones at home!

What you will need:

- Large cardboard tube (a gift wrap tube or a paper towel tube)
- Large plastic bowl
- Stirrer (to mix the flour glue)
- Flour
- Water
- Newspaper or brown paper bags
- Masking tape
- White, yellow, or tan tempera paint
- Brush

Before you begin, ask an adult to make simple thin glue from flour and water. Mix 1 cup of flour into 1 cup of water until the mixture is thin and runny. Stir it into 4 cups of boiling water. Simmer for about 3 minutes and then cool.

Crumble newspaper into two balls. Tape a ball to each end of the cardboard tube. Tear strips of newspaper and/or brown bag paper. You'll need a lot of strips! Dip a newspaper strip into the cooled glue and then wrap it around the dinosaur bone. Cover the ends and the tube—the entire bone. Allow the bone to dry completely and then paint it!

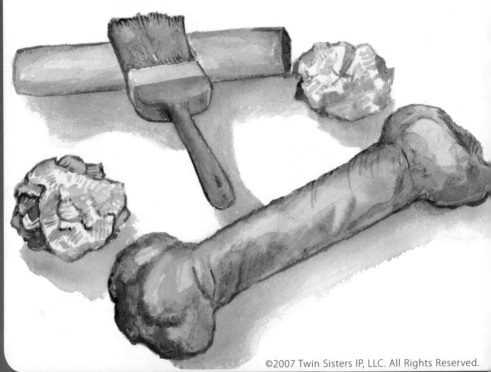

©2007 Twin Sisters IP, LLC. All Rights Reserved.

Dinosaur Feet

You'll need two empty tissue boxes that are the same size. Cut and glue in place a piece of cardboard or posterboard that fits inside the openings of each box to make them smaller so your feet will stay inside of them. Paint the boxes and allow them to dry. You can also cover the boxes with construction paper. Remember, no one knows the colors of the dinosaurs! Make toenails by cutting out triangles from construction paper or craft foam. Glue them in place. Once the glue has dried, try on your new dinosaur feet!

Dinosaur Eggs

Before you begin, ask an adult to make simple thin glue from flour and water. Mix 1 cup of flour into 1 cup of water until the mixture is thin and runny. Stir it into 4 cups of boiling water. Simmer for about 3 minutes and then cool.

Blow up a large balloon. Tear strips of newspaper and/or brown paper bag. You'll need a lot of strips! Dip a newspaper strip into the cooled glue and then wrap it around the balloon. Let the dinosaur egg dry for a few days. When the egg is dry, you can pop the balloon and remove it from inside the egg. Decorate the egg with paint or markers. Remember that no one knows the color of the dinosaurs' eggs!

©2007 Twin Sisters IP, LLC. All Rights Reserved.

Gridlock

Solve each riddle by reading the grid coordinates and filling in the letters on the blanks below. The first number in the coordinate tells you how many columns over the letter will be. (Follow the blue numbers below the grid.) The second number tells you how many rows up the letter will be. (Follow the green numbers that go up the side of the grid.)

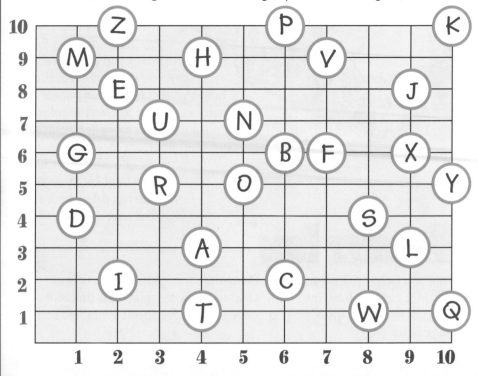

1. What do you call a Triceratops that fell down the stairs?

‾‾
___ ___ ___ ___   ___ ___ ___ ___
1:4 2:2 5:7 5:5   8:4 4:3 3:7 3:5

2. How long should a dinosaur's legs be?

___ ___ ___ ___   ___ ___ ___ ___ ___ ___   ___ ___
9:3 5:5 5:7 1:6   2:8 5:7 5:5 3:7 1:6 4:9   4:1 5:5

___ ___ ___ ___ ___   ___ ___ ___   ___ ___ ___ ___ ___ ___
3:3 2:8 4:3 6:2 4:9   4:1 4:9 2:8   1:6 3:5 5:5 3:7 5:7 1:4

3. What do you call a scared Tyrannosaurus rex?

___   ___ ___ ___ ___ ___ ___ ___   ___ ___ ___
4:3   5:7 2:8 3:5 7:9 5:5 3:7 8:4   3:5 2:8 9:6

Solutions - pg. 26

©2007 Twin Sisters IP, LLC. All Rights Reserved.

Gridlock

4. What do you get when you cross a dinosaur with a lemon?

$\underline{\hspace{1cm}}$ $\underline{\hspace{1cm}}$ $\underline{\hspace{1cm}}$ $\underline{\hspace{1cm}}$ $\overline{\underline{\hspace{1cm}}}$ $\underline{\hspace{1cm}}$ $\underline{\hspace{1cm}}$ $\underline{\hspace{1cm}}$ $\underline{\hspace{1cm}}$

4:3   1:4 2:2 5:7 5:5   8:4 5:5 3:7 3:5

5. What was Tyrannosaurus rex's favorite number?

$\underline{\hspace{1cm}}$ $\underline{\hspace{1cm}}$ $\underline{\hspace{1cm}}$ $\underline{\hspace{1cm}}$ $\underline{\hspace{1cm}}$ ($\underline{\hspace{1cm}}$ $\underline{\hspace{1cm}}$ $\underline{\hspace{1cm}}$)

2:8 2:2 1:6 4:9 4:1   4:3 4:1 2:8

6. What do you get when you cross a dinosaur with fireworks?

$\underline{\hspace{1cm}}$ $\underline{\hspace{1cm}}$ $\underline{\hspace{1cm}}$ $\underline{\hspace{1cm}}$ $\underline{\hspace{1cm}}$ $\underline{\hspace{1cm}}$ $\underline{\hspace{1cm}}$ $\underline{\hspace{1cm}}$

1:4 2:2 5:7 5:5 1:9 2:2 4:1 2:8

7. What do you get if you cross a Triceratops with a kangaroo?

$\underline{\hspace{1cm}}$ $\underline{\hspace{1cm}}$ $\underline{\hspace{1cm}}$ $\underline{\hspace{1cm}}$ $\underline{\hspace{1cm}}$ $\underline{\hspace{1cm}}$ $\underline{\hspace{1cm}}$ $\overline{\underline{\hspace{1cm}}}$ $\underline{\hspace{1cm}}$ $\underline{\hspace{1cm}}$ $\underline{\hspace{1cm}}$ $\underline{\hspace{1cm}}$

4:1 3:5 2:2 6:2 2:8 3:5 4:3   4:9 5:5 6:10 8:4

8. What did dinosaurs have that no other animals ever had?

$\underline{\hspace{1cm}}$ $\underline{\hspace{1cm}}$ $\underline{\hspace{1cm}}$ $\underline{\hspace{1cm}}$ $\underline{\hspace{1cm}}$ $\underline{\hspace{1cm}}$ $\underline{\hspace{1cm}}$ $\underline{\hspace{1cm}}$ $\underline{\hspace{1cm}}$ $\underline{\hspace{1cm}}$ $\underline{\hspace{1cm}}$ $\underline{\hspace{1cm}}$

6:6 4:3 6:6 10:5   1:4 2:2 5:7 5:5 8:4 4:3 3:7 3:5 8:4

9. What makes more noise than a dinosaur?

$\underline{\hspace{1cm}}$ $\underline{\hspace{1cm}}$ $\underline{\hspace{1cm}}$ $\underline{\hspace{1cm}}$ $\underline{\hspace{1cm}}$ $\underline{\hspace{1cm}}$ $\underline{\hspace{1cm}}$ $\underline{\hspace{1cm}}$ $\underline{\hspace{1cm}}$ $\underline{\hspace{1cm}}$ $\underline{\hspace{1cm}}$

4:1 8:1 5:5   1:4 2:2 5:7 5:5 8:4 4:3 3:7 3:5 8:4

10. What do you call a dinosaur that left its armor out in the rain?

$\underline{\hspace{1cm}}$ $\underline{\hspace{1cm}}$ $\underline{\hspace{1cm}}$ $\underline{\hspace{1cm}}$ $\underline{\hspace{1cm}}$ $\underline{\hspace{1cm}}$ $\underline{\hspace{1cm}}$ $\underline{\hspace{1cm}}$ $\overline{\underline{\hspace{1cm}}}$ $\underline{\hspace{1cm}}$ $\underline{\hspace{1cm}}$ $\underline{\hspace{1cm}}$ $\underline{\hspace{1cm}}$

4:3   8:4 4:1 2:8 1:6 5:5 8:4 4:3 3:7   3:5 3:7 8:4 4:1

2007 Twin Sisters IP, LLC. All Rights Reserved.

Name Those Prehistoric Reptiles!

Solutions - pg. 26

1 _____

2 _____

3 _____

4 _____

5 _____

6 _____

©2007 Twin Sisters IP, LLC. All Rights Reserved.

Name Those Prehistoric Reptiles!

Solutions - pg. 26

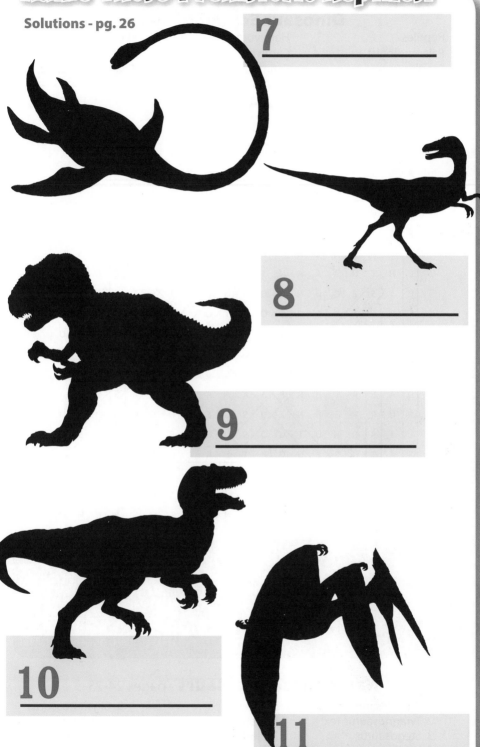

7 _____

8 _____

9 _____

10 _____

11 _____

©2007 Twin Sisters IP, LLC. All Rights Reserved.

Answer Page

Dinosaur Scramble - page 4

Reptiles	Herbivore	Biped
Paleontologist	Carnivore	Quadruped
Fossils	Extinct	Fearfully Great Lizard

Prehistoric Dig - page 18

```
O  E  S  I  O  O  H  A  L  L  O  S  A  U  N  A  D  I  O  N
U  O  O  P  L  E  S  I  O  S  A  U  R  U  S  E  S  A  P  L
A  L  T  B  E  C  O  M  P  S  O  G  N  A  T  H  U  S  T  I
X  U  T  Y  R  A  N  N  O  S  A  U  R  U  S  R  E  X  E  A
B  P  G  U  R  S  G  O  A  S  S  O  T  N  N  S  U  R  R
R  I  T  I  I  A  I  S  L  S  L  R  A  U  T  S  R  A  U
A  C  A  S  G  R  N  I  G  G  L  U  R  A  O  T  S  N  U
C  H  T  U  A  A  A  N  T  A  A  O  S  U  L  S  E  A  O  U
I  T  S  Z  Q  U  N  G  O  S  N  O  S  T  E  T  G  L  T  C
H  H  T  A  H  S  O  O  O  S  I  O  A  A  N  A  O  T  R  T
O  Y  R  U  L  L  N  I  T  H  A  O  T  U  U  I  S  O  A  U
S  O  I  S  N  T  S  C  C  O  C  U  R  O  T  R  A  G  T  U
A  S  C  S  O  E  O  A  H  L  S  U  R  P  S  U  U  C  R  R
U  A  E  R  L  H  R  P  A  A  A  M  U  P  A  R  S  N  A
R  U  R  P  S  B  N  Z  U  S  G  E  U  O  S  U  U  O  D  O
U  I  A  Q  H  U  T  U  O  S  D  U  G  R  P  A  S  R  S  R
S  A  T  U  B  E  U  G  P  T  E  R  A  N  O  D  O  N  U  L
S  O  O  O  U  P  E  T  R  I  C  E  R  A  T  B  R  C  M  S
A  S  P  Q  I  T  I  C  H  T  H  Y  O  S  A  U  R  U  S  B
U  O  S  A  S  U  R  O  O  U  N  U  U  T  O  S  R  R  H  U
```

Gridlock - pages 22-23

1. Dino-sore
2. Long enough to reach the ground
3. A nervous rex
4. A dino-sour
5. Eight (ate)
6. Dinomite
7. Tricera-hops
8. Baby dinosaurs!
9. Two dinosaurs
10. A Stegosau-rust!

Name Those Dinosaurs - pages 24-25

1. Brachiosaurus
2. Tyrannosaurus rex
3. Stegosaurus
4. Ichthyosaurus
5. Triceratops
6. Pteranodon
7. Plesiosaurus
8. Compsognathus
9. Giganotosaurus
10. Allosaurus
11. Quetzalcoatlus

©2007 Twin Sisters IP, LLC. All Rights Reserved.